We Can Do Better

Setting the Pace for the Next Generation

We Can Do Better

Setting the Pace for the Next Generation

D. Jomo

Anchor Book Press • Palatine

We Can Do Better:
Setting the Pace for the Next Generation
Copyright © Daphne Jomo 2023
Anchor Book Press
440 W Colfax Street, Unit 1132, Palatine, IL 60078
ISBN: 9781958992050
Scripture References: KJV
Printed in the United States

Dedication

This book is dedicated to my beloved family, for their patience, love, and support through this journey. For all the times I seemed absent and distanced, I thank you for your understanding.

Preface

In my search for community, to understand the true meaning of my existence and purpose, I had enrolled in a four-year Education for Ministry program with the University of the South Sewance in 2016. And—no—I wasn't preparing for the priesthood, a goal my teasing friends suggested. As the fourth and final year of my program approached, I pondered my journey and wondered how I could be a doer, and not just a listener.

The path to priesthood or ordained ministry is one that requires dedication and complete sacrifice—and I don't see myself wearing that shoe anytime soon, if at all. And if one day I do, I will do so with a full understanding of whatever ministry I am called to. The men and women who do this take up a huge responsibility and I do not take it lightly at all.

I had been warned that there would be a heavy regimen of reading and religious history studies to measure my commitment and readiness, which in fact I took lightly. That is until I had to flip through 3000 years of church history. Needless to say, church history is intertwined with the world's history and included an extensive history of Islam.

It was a study of major shifts in religious history. It included a review of the Roman Empire's transition to Christianity, the emergence of the Muslim religion, the Crusades that prompted Europeans to invade Muslim-controlled lands, and the Reformation of the church by theologians such as Martin Luther and John Calvin.

It was a program built around mentorship and interfaith dialogue. Each session ending with an in-depth theological reflection. Every individual brought his or her own unique understanding of the world we live in, and each brought their belief in the existence of a supernatural being somewhere in the universe, and each brought their doubts of different religious beliefs as everyone felt their opinion was valid. This necessarily resulted in the questioning of the faith of others as many opinions are mutually exclusive. However, each of us was committed to respecting the opinions of everyone in the group.

What fascinated me was the unity and love that we shared by the end of the year, even with our differences of beliefs and values. Our community grew stronger, and we felt more comfortable among ourselves. We shared meals together, shared personal life experiences, and built life-long relationships.

The lesson that I learned from this little community was that we can accept each other for who we are, we can listen with an intent to understand others, and we can give support to others who do not share our beliefs. We grew stronger each year and I noticed how a clearer understanding of my role in community dissipated some of the negative notions about the people in other religious groups. I was finally free to share my love for all people, even those who were different than I was.

My final year was affected by the pandemic and meetings moved online. However, we maintained the dialogue online through the pandemic until my graduation in

May 2020. A few months later I began facilitating an interfaith social justice dialogue group, which was organized by my church. We need more open dialogue so that we are able to work together. We need to determine how to work through the problems that linger in our society.

This book is in no way dogmatic. It was written to provoke dialogue and action. I am still on a journey to learn more about existing in a peaceful world regardless of race, gender, religion, or economic status. I hope that after you read this book, you will also be hungry for more in-depth understanding of all communities you are a part of. whether a nuclear family, a workplace environment, a church, a country, or the world.

Table of Contents

Introduction

The recent pandemic took a terrible toll on the world as we scrambled to find answers, among them a vaccine and a cure. I could go on and on listing the negative effects and I do list some in this book, but what I want to concentrate on is how this pandemic was an education. It was educational in the sense that it made me, and many others, look at the world we live in, to really see the problems. Some problems were created specifically by the pandemic, but others had been here all along with most people giving them very little consideration, much less putting forth any effort to find solutions.

In this book, I hope to bring to light some of those problems and some solutions because I am convinced, we can do better. I will offer some ideas and I am sure you will have some of your own. Most of us can do better even if we are already aware of some issues. Almost all of these problems will take time to correct. If there were a fast-fix, those of you who already knew about the problems would have already fixed them. Secondly, these are the problems that caught my attention. I am sure, as you read you might think of others. Maybe the ones I mention will bring the others to mind or maybe you were already wondering what you could do about various problems. This book is not meant to be the end all solution. Rather, I hope that it helps you to see little problems in your neighborhood that you can solve. I hope it helps you see bigger problems and how we need to work together to solve the bigger issues.

For the most part, I answer the questions from my point of view, but the whole idea is that you improve upon them and come up with your own ideas. Ideas that work for you. Ideas that work for your community and the world.

Chapter One
The Beginning

As life happens there are tons of ups and downs. It's a journey of discovery – there are moments of mountaintops and moments in the deep valley of despair.

Rick Warren

While ups and downs are a part of everyone's journey, how you face it makes you the person or artiste you are.

Jubin Nautiyal

The beginning. The first case of Corona virus was reported in December 2019 in Wuhan, China. On January 20, 2020, the first case was reported in the United States. Then on January 30th the World Health Organization (WHO) declared it an outbreak, a public health emergency of concern. On February 11, WHO named the virus COVID-19. The first community spread was documented on February 2. By March 11 of 2020, WHO declared that Corona virus was a global pandemic.

I remember March 5, 2020. That was the day that I began

to personally experience the pandemic. Before that day it was mainly something out there that was happening to other people that I did not know, that were not in my area. I was not really concerned or paying too much attention to what was happening. On this day, I looked through my office window and saw a Princess Cruise ship near the San Francisco port. That was weird, I thought. The sight of a Princess Cruise was common from my office vantage point. I frequently saw passengers boarding or getting off cruise ships. But this time, the ship was not docked. It was moored a short distance from the dock—and I wondered why.

Later, I took a walk to the lobby. There, I heard a news report that state officials had decided the ship would not be allowed to dock for 14 days. Officials wanted to be sure that any passengers infected with the dangerous virus would not have contact with the general public while they were still contagious. This got my attention. Cruise ships' passengers were being detained. This is America! We don't just detain people who are not suspected of illegal activities. This must be important!

As the days went by, I was still grappling with events happening all over the world at this time. Every day I would use my phone to record the ship at sea because this is what we do in the 21st century. We document events by recording a video on our phones. On one occasion, I saw a helicopter hovering over the ship and dropping something onboard. Watching the news later that day, I learned they had dropped essential supplies, food, water, and toiletries, for the passengers and crew. Stunned, I turned to a co-worker and asked, "Is this really happening?" It was early in the pandemic, and I still could not get my head around the idea that this was major. Nor did I realize how life-changing it would be for all of us; this was just the beginning.

"It's a pandemic," my colleague said. I asked what does that even mean? I remember her trying to explain, but other than this cruise ship moored off the dock, I really didn't have much interest and it didn't make much difference to me. I had not lived through a pandemic and did not grasp the seriousness of the situation. While I felt bad for everyone on that ship, the numbers were still just numbers to me and not people in my mind and experience.

My time and energy were taken up with things that were more pressing to me. Here I was, a new small business owner. My clientele had doubled between January and February of 2020, and I needed more employees. I had posted a notice to hire new employees and I was interviewing prospects at that time. Given all the attention on the news and the apparent danger, I wasn't sure whether to cancel the interviews or continue interviewing? The reality of the pandemic hadn't hit yet. It just felt surreal, like it was just a story from a movie.

A few days later, I learned that three people on the ship had the virus and one person had died from the disease. This was hitting a little closer to home. Now, even though I didn't personally know the deceased, he was in my neighborhood. He was no longer just a number to me. The threat of the virus was becoming real.

There were news stories of many people in the United States that were dying. There were warnings that those with underlying conditions were at higher risk. Those over 60 were included in those reported to be at a higher risk of dying from the infection. Everyday had something new and neither I nor anyone I had conversations with understood what was ahead of us. We had no idea that one year later, in 2021, we would still be sheltering in place from the pandemic. I remember canceling the scheduled job interviews; I remember the office zoom call where everyone was asked to stay home. I remember feeling so frustrated. I was also afraid—so fearful that my friends had to do my grocery shopping.

I watched the city government renting hotel rooms for the homeless people on the street. I recall neighbors helping neighbors, the elderly, and the vulnerable. I watched the news as Italy flew its flag at half-staff to mourn Italian victims of the pandemic. I recall Spain recording 849 deaths within 24 hours. These events were jaw-dropping and unsettling. It was like nothing I had ever experienced, and it was getting my attention.

I picked up my phone and called family and friends and everyone I could think of to warn them of the deadly virus, even those I am not close to, knowing that not everyone watches the news like I do. As a believer and follower of Christ, I am obligated to live by example and doing so meant that I not only think of myself in times of adversity but those around me. Spurred by the worsening conditions and the uplifting news stories of people who were making a difference, I kept asking myself, "What could I do to help?"

April 2020, four weeks after the shelter in place mandate, I woke up to a text on my phone from a friend, "Just an FYI, I tested positive for the virus." I lay on my bed trying to understand the implications for me. The implications of a text from someone with whom I had recently been in close contact. I am not one to generally fear or worry about news of ill health, but I usually ask for a prognosis and treatment plan. However, with COVID-19, no one seemed to know what was going on. The course of the disease was so incredibly different from person to person. It was so new, there was no acceptable standard of care or treatment. There was no reliable prognosis or treatment. So, I lay in bed flipping through channels trying to get as much information as I could while I wondered what this meant for my health, personally, as well as my friend. Just how sick would she become? Would she recover? Would I become infected? Would I recover if I became infected? I wanted a prognosis and a treatment plan for my friend and for myself, if needed.

So, I locked myself inside and contacted my family to let them know that I had been in contact with someone who had COVID-19. My dad cried on the phone like it was the last time he was going to be speaking to me. I lay in bed unable to close my eyes with the fear that I might not wake up. It didn't help that the person I came in contact with had a more severe case than most people in her age group and health status. Each day I woke up I asked myself if today was the day it was going to happen? Is this the day I would end up in the ICU?

Waking up every day was a blessing that I was now acutely aware of. Coincidentally, my annual checkup was scheduled for the next day. The test came back positive. My doctor called three days later to inform me and to discuss my positive result. She asked that I quarantine for 14 days to help slow down the spread of the virus. Given that this was the start of the pandemic, I got calls from my team of health providers almost daily and the health department as well. It was a terrifying experience. For the next 14 days, I sat on my bed flipping through the news channels. I read books and I started writing this book.

I was asymptomatic and getting by each day until I lost my

sense of taste. Then I panicked. I tried out different foods but tasted nothing. Even so, I was lucky to have people who shopped for me and dropped off food at my door. Most of whom I had no personal relationship. In fact, one of the individuals who checked up on me daily was just an acquaintance I waved at occasionally. We were not the same age or race. But daily she messaged me, and she went out of her way for me. We became good friends because of this situation.

At times like this we feel the urge to pause, take a deep breath, and ask what really matters in our life and our society. Life had been moving at such a rapid a pace that many of us had not been considering what is necessary and important in life. Situations like this often cause us to slow down and review our priorities.

The irony of the pandemic is that it has helped some of us who lived with a self-centered mindset to realize our obligations to each other. Stories of good deeds were all over the news. We called them heroic acts, even though such deeds should be considered the norm. And we recognized our need to help.

As I wrote I recognized that I really did not know the best way to channel my thoughts and the energy that flowed within me so that the message would be well perceived. My hope was to create an awareness of needs that should be addressed and supply some ideas of what we can do individually, nationally, and globally. I don't claim to have all the answers but as a group we can make a difference in our world. Looking back, we can see that in times of crisis people are much more likely to rise to the demands of the situation. History is full of examples when people have prevailed against the odds. We have not always done so perfectly, and we won't do it perfectly now, but we can improve. We can do better.

In this crisis, questions about the meaning of life were on my mind on a daily basis. Faced with our mortality, we are often more in tune with what is really important in life. What is the yardstick for living a fulfilled life in an irrational and chaotic world? In the end, it will be different for each individual as we all have different abilities and resources. As a Christian, I feel God has given us all gifts and talents which will determine the areas in which we serve others. In this book, I try to present a wide variety of options knowing some people feel led to serve the elderly, while others see the needs of children, or those in poverty. The important goal is that we must not fail to understand that we live together as a diverse people with strengths and weaknesses. We need to strike a balance between our self-interests and the needs of our neighbor, our country, and our world. We are like a tree with branches that flourish from the root but if the root is not watered or nurtured eventually the entire tree will suffer. The impact will not be immediate, but as the damaged roots fails to thrive, it will be unable to contribute to the health of the tree. One day, we will wake up to a dead tree.

The pandemic threatens all of us—regardless of nationality, race, party, or income. COVID-19 did a lot to remind us of our dependence on others for our existence as an interconnected group. The pandemic did a lot to help many people recapture their sense of priorities and values, to realize that the most important things in life cannot be bought.

During COVID-19, we saw examples of the selfless acts of many televised to the whole world, people coming together with one common goal—to defeat COVID-19. I have seen and heard tremendous stories of good deeds and read peoples' reaction to them. News stations that normally ignored good deeds as unnewsworthy have broadcast these stories which became newsworthy due to their connection to the pandemic. This book will provide accounts of some stories that caught my attention while I was quarantined and during the remaining period of the pandemic and how it changed my perspective of the world.

Chapter Two
Essential Workers

"I feel a very unusual sensation – if it is not indigestion, I think it must be gratitude."
Benjamin Disraeli

Sudden Hoorays for Healers

On March 20th, a few days after the state government ordered Californians to *shelter-in-place*, an emergency room doctor's wife tweeted "we just made the difficult decision for him to isolate and move into our garage apartment for the foreseeable future as he continues to treat patients" (Caitlin, 2020).

The same month, another doctor, Tiffany Osborn, made a tough decision to move into a camper parked outside her home in St. Louis to keep her family safe and will live there for the next year, joining her family back inside in March 2021. So many doctors and hospital staff followed suit with some finding alternative homes for their families while they stayed home ((Zdanowicz, 2021).

As if the daily hassle of dealing with patients and trying to combat the virus wasn't enough, these doctors also had to sacrifice their families to stay on the forefront. News like this became ubiquitous on TV screens during the pandemic and it was truly heartwarming to see. Prior to this time, I never gave much thought to the danger faced by healthcare workers when treating patients with highly infectious diseases. Even today, I do not know what precautions those doctors take to keep their families safe. Only the pandemic made the precautions during COVID newsworthy.

We are once again reminded that getting into the medical profession is like signing or swearing an oath to humanity, "with special obligations to human beings, those sound of mind and body as well as the infirm." The Hippocratic Oath has been around for many years, outlining the responsibility of the medical profession. In current practice, not every doctor takes this oath, but some may take a similar oath depending on the current practice in their personal situation. Over the years, there have been changes and different versions and even entirely different oaths, but the overall concept remains the same:

> *I swear to fulfill, to the best of my ability and judgment, this covenant:*
>
> *I will respect the hard-won scientific gains of those physicians in whose steps I walk, and gladly share such knowledge as is mine with those who are to follow.*
>
> *I will apply, for the benefit of the sick, all measures that are required, avoiding those twin traps of over-treatment and therapeutic nihilism.*

I will remember that there is art to medicine as well as science, and that warmth, sympathy, and understanding may outweigh the surgeon's knife or the chemist's drug.

I will not be ashamed to say, "I know not," nor will I fail to call in my colleagues when the skills of another are needed for a patient's recovery.

I will respect the privacy of my patients, for their problems are not disclosed to me that the world may know. Most especially must I tread with care in matters of life and death. If it is given me to save a life, all thanks. But it may also be within my power to take a life; this awesome responsibility must be faced with great humbleness and awareness of my own frailty. Above all, I must not play at God.

I will remember that I do not treat a fever chart, a cancerous growth, but a sick human being, whose illness may affect the person's family and economic stability. My responsibility includes these related problems, if I am to care adequately for the sick.

I will prevent disease whenever I can, for prevention is preferable to cure.

I will remember that I remain a member of society, with special obligations to all my fellow human beings, those sound of mind and body as well as the infirm.

If I do not violate this oath, may I enjoy life and art, respected while I live and remembered with affection thereafter. May I always act so as to preserve the finest traditions of my calling, and may I long experience the joy of healing those who seek my help.

The Nightingale Pledge, modified from the "Hippocratic Oath" and composed by Lystra E. Gretter in 1893, is often pledged by nurses:

I solemnly pledge myself before God and in the presence of this assembly to pass my life in purity and to practice my profession faithfully.

I will abstain from whatever is deleterious and mischievous and will not take or knowingly administer any harmful drug.

I will do all in my power to maintain and elevate the standard of my profession and will hold in confidence all personal matters committed to my keeping and all family affairs coming to my knowledge in the practice of my calling.

With loyalty will I aid the physician in his work, and as a missioner of health, I will dedicate myself to devoted service for human welfare.

https://nursing.vanderbilt.edu/news/flo
rence-nightingale-pledge/

Question

Were you aware of the details of these oaths? Did either bring out responsibilities of medical practitioners that you were not aware of?

For me personally, it emphasized the fact that medical professionals are accepting a lot more responsibility toward others than I have in my profession. I personally was not aware of the depth or seriousness of this oath and had not taken time to read it pre-pandemic. I did not even know that there was an oath for nursing.

The men and women who take these oaths are to me among the most selfless beings on earth. I admire their strength and courage to "first do no harm" and ensure to the best of their knowledge that they do everything possible to "prevent disease whenever they can."

While some may think that the high salaries of the medical profession adequately compensate for the responsibility, I have to remind you that many healthcare professionals are not making huge salaries. Take your family doctor, most are middle income, with years of college debt. That is true for nurses and other support personnel as well.

The recent reminder on TV about the sacrifices these medical practitioners made just a few days into the shelter-in-place was hard to ignore.

Understanding *appreciation.* - The Oxford Dictionary defines appreciation as the "feeling of being grateful for something ..." Sometimes it takes a crisis for appreciation to come to light. I have always been aware of the importance of doctors in our communities, but despite my awareness, I have never been as grateful as I am for these professionals as I have been since the pandemic. Even while the pandemic raged and the news called them heroes, little did I consider that a certain subset of the medical profession has always put their life on the line in dealing with contagious patients that have conditions other than coronavirus.

Question

How can we show appreciation to healthcare providers?

SEND A FLOWER OR A THANK YOU NOTE TO YOUR DOCTOR. Recently I received mail from the hospital where I received care and it said, "let your team of care providers know you appreciate them." It had an envelope to send a check, gift card, flowers, etc. I was happy to see that they were doing that. I have been with them for about five years, and this was the first time I received such mail. This I think is a good incentive as appreciation often goes a long way in improving performance and the mental health of the care providers.

Appreciation has benefits for the patient, as well. Research has shown that appreciation improves performance. It is in the best interest of everyone that these professionals are emotionally prepared to go above and beyond the requirements of duty. These medical professionals have given their best, sacrificed their lives, and sometimes, put the lives of their families at risk during a pandemic. They leave home every day not knowing what each day holds. Let's be sure to show our appreciation.

What does the post-pandemic era hold for them? Do we forget their contributions? Do we forget that there are other contagious and deadly diseases they are more likely to come in contact with that the average person? Will we continue to honor them after the pandemic ends?

Essential Workers Redefined Amidst the Pandemic

Janitors, grocery store employees, and warehouse workers are now considered essential workers. One of the positive things that happened during the shelter-in-place was the redefinition of essential workers. This redefinition occurred when city governments identified groups of workers who needed to be on-the-job during pandemic-related shutdowns.

On April 8th, Juju Chan of ABC News broadcast a report that put a spotlight on service workers and sacrifices made by workers that I had never considered essential prior to the pandemic. Not because I thought they weren't essential, but just because I never thought about it. At the end of the segment, one essential worker—a janitor that cleans hospital rooms—said, "I hope we can remain visible and appreciated after the pandemic." I admire those people who, prior to the pandemic, treated the custodian with the same respect higher level colleagues were treated. We've probably all read biographies of important people who said things like, "My mother taught me to respect the custodian, to know his name, and to acknowledge his presence." Hopefully, the pandemic has helped all of us to realize the importance of this mindset toward essential workers that are considered inferior by some.

During the pandemic, we were suddenly seeing videos of people showing appreciation to essential workers. This suddenly became newsworthy only because it was attached to the pandemic. The topic on news outlet and social media pages was swiftly driven by a new awareness. The US department of Homeland Security defined essential workers as, "those who conduct a range of operations and services that are typically essential to continue critical infrastructure operations."

People who fall into this category are essential because we cannot do without their services. Many of the people in our essential workforce are those who are the least-paid with the least respected jobs like grocery store clerks, fast-food employees, and janitors. Prior to the pandemic, I had never thought of these workers as essential. Again, not because I thought they weren't, but because I did not think about it. Even now, there is the tendency to think they were essential because of the pandemic, but if we stop to think about it, they have always been and will always be essential. The pandemic was not what made them essential. The pandemic served to enlighten us of the need for and importance of these essential workers.

The pandemic made me aware of the dangers people in these categories encounter and how they sacrifice their own health and endanger their families and loved ones to be on the frontline in keeping the economy running. Some states mandated an additional hazard-pay or hero-pay for grocery workers working during the pandemic. This did create other problems for those with limited income as stores raised prices and reduced employee hours to compensate for the lost income caused by higher wages. It seems we are willing to pay more for electronics than groceries. The electronic industry has a profit margin around 50% while the grocery industry has a profit margin between 1% and 3%.

Question

Why did it take the pandemic for me to recognize the importance of the essential workers in the community?

I asked a group of individuals their definition of essential worker prior to the pandemic. Here are some of their responses:

Response 1:

> *Prior to pandemic I always thought essential workers were doctors, nurses, paramedics, police, and the people who maintained civic structures, such as, electricity and garbage collection, etc. Now I see the list of essential workers is actually much broader, from supermarket cashiers to truck drivers to factory workers to food delivery folks, etc. The people with no prior expectation of being deemed essential, yet there they were, risking infection from COVID so the rest of us could safely shelter.*

Response 2:

> *I hadn't thought that much about essential workers except to imagine these are people we can't live without and couldn't live without during the COVID lockdown.*
>
> *They include sanitation workers, health care workers, food services workers,*

firefighters, police, and workers who take care of downed power lines and all other dangerous public situations.

Response 3:

Before the pandemic, I would have said there are two groups of people who are essential workers. People who work in hospitals and doctor's offices, because healthcare is essential to survival. People who drive mass transit. A few years ago, BART (Bay Area Rapid Transit) had a strike and a politician over in the East Bay said BART workers can't strike because mass transit is essential for us to survive.

I confess I never thought about people who work in grocery stores or drugstores. Since the pandemic, I realize they are essential too.

Response 4:

I don't remember hearing the term essential worker before the pandemic began. If I had heard the term before March 2020, I would have assumed that it referred to someone who was the key to getting something done in the workplace, because of their knowledge, or specific skills that no one else in the workplace had, mostly those in supervisory positions would have come to mind.

In other words, without that one person, the mission of the business would not be accomplished. And other people wouldn't be able to do their jobs. Perhaps one essential person had the password to a system that needed to be used to operate the business. Or even on a more basic level, they had the keys to open the business' doors. That was my perspective.

Question

Will we continue to give these groups the credit they deserve after the pandemic is over? What can we do to show our appreciation for the essential workers around us?

SAY THANK YOU AND CHECK IN! Making it a habit to be aware of how you treat essential workers is important. Be courteous and take a moment to get to know the name of the custodian and clerk that you walk by every day or the security officer in front of your apartment or office building. It makes a difference. It doesn't take a lot of effort on our part to make a person feel that they are appreciated. In addition to those we consider essential, we should treat everyone with respect by being courteous and friendly.

Since coming to awareness of this group of essential workers, I now take my time to say thank you to essential workers around me. I spend time chatting with them. One of the custodians stops by when she makes her rounds in the morning to tell me about her struggles with taking her kids to day care before work or other childcare issues. Another just likes to wave and smile a lot; it has become our daily routine. When I come back to the office after a few days of absence, I often mention where I've been. The pandemic made me appreciate people more and take a few minutes to chat with the people I see every day.

I recently stopped to ask a security officer if he was okay or if he needed someone to talk to. A few minutes earlier, I looked his way and thought I saw tears rolling down his cheek as I hurried to my destination. I couldn't help but ask. And he responded, "I'm okay Ms. Dee, it's just my allergies. It's very windy today and my eyes just can't handle that sometimes. Thank you for asking, thanks for noticing." Indeed, it was windy, and he was genuinely grateful I asked, saying thank you over and over. I noticed his demeanor changed after that day. He seemed to have more energy and he smiled each time he saw me approach or walk by to the office. Sometimes when he was far away, he would rush over or shout out, "Good morning Ms. Dee." When I didn't go to the office for months, upon returning he said, "It's good to see you Ms. Dee, I was worried and hoping you were okay because of the virus. I prayed for God to keep you safe." In that moment I felt appreciated and that my presence mattered to this individual. It is ironic that in trying to show appreciation for others, I in turn was shown respect and concern. Knowing that someone else cared made a difference for me, too.

In making others feel loved, appreciated, and fulfilled, we are also helping ourselves. There is no better feeling than knowing our actions have made a difference for someone. In turn, we often find someone is looking out for us each day. We never fully understand the power of our actions and what they may mean to a person who finds comfort because of how we treat them.

Knowing how important these people are in our community, let's take a moment to consider some ways to show appreciation.

SHOP AT YOUR LOCAL MOM & POP GROCERY STORE DOWN THE STREET - Let your local mom and pop store that stayed open for you all through the pandemic know that you are grateful that they stayed open. If possible, patronize them more. In doing so, we show our appreciation and often times develop a personal relationship. While they may not replace your favorite big box store, you can appreciate the difference. The local store is run by people you can develop a relationship with, and the big box store is a business.

I used to shop at the big grocery stores pre-pandemic and barely went to the store on my street, just outside my building. The first three months of the pandemic, stores were running out of food, cleaning supplies, and home goods. So, whenever I made my way to the store, I was spending hundreds of dollars filling my cart with both things that I needed and things I thought I might need in fear not finding the products when I really did need them. The grocery store lines were long and could go down an entire block as stores in my area only allowed a few people in at a time to practice social distancing. I decided to go to the grocery store very early in the morning to beat the line, but it seemed like everyone else was thinking what I was thinking. Often, the shelves were mostly empty when I arrived.

On one occasion, after uselessly going to several stores including Target and Costco to find toilet paper, I was frustrated. That was the beginning of online shopping for me. But Amazon was out of toilet paper that could be delivered immediately; meaning I could order through

Amazon, but delivery would be 7 – 10 days later. Desperate to get toilet papers ASAP, I walked into the small mom & pop shop just outside my building and was blown away to see a shelf full of toilet paper. I asked the store owner, "How is this possible? Where did you get all this toilet paper? I have been looking for toilet paper for days." He replied, "Really, we've had toilet paper for a while. I have more in storage." He had a wide grin on his face like "it's just a toilet paper, why are you so excited." I thought, they clearly haven't been watching the news. I decided to use the opportunity to look around the store for other items that I needed. This was the end of my standing in line at the grocery store. This mom-and-pop store was a gem and a life-saver for me. They had almost everything that I needed, and I only ordered what they didn't have from Amazon or Instacart.

The store was run by the owners who were very friendly. If I needed something they didn't carry, all I had to do was ask and they would order it and fill the shelves. They simply asked me, "Is the product good? What do you like about it? Okay, we will start carrying it. Come next week and it will be here." With time, I barely shopped anywhere else. They had fruits, vegetables, frozen foods, cereal, drinks, alcohol, almost everything I needed. Even better, they have two additional staff members that work with them, one in the morning and one in the evening. Each time I see them at the store, we catch up about life, the pandemic, and my shopping experience. My relationship with the store owners has progressed to the point where they told me I could call them for anything I need if I'm sick and can't make it to the store. They will deliver. Mind you, they don't normally deliver. Because it's a small store they do not have the staff to offer delivery to all customers.

Question

How can we develop relationships with small business owners?

ACKNOWLEDGMENT AND APPRECIATION! - For me personally, when I walk into the store, I am upbeat and chatty, as I acknowledge their presence. I help them improve the quality of goods they have on the shelf by repeatedly shopping at the store, engaging in conversation with them, and letting them know about other products I want. I often point out expired goods on the shelf, calling them to their attention so they can get rid of them. I ask how they are dealing with the pandemic and talk about business setbacks due to the pandemic and the economy. The owner and staff feel seen and appreciated. One interesting thing, by the seventh month of the pandemic, I would walk into the store and see people lined up to make a purchase. The store had never had lines before. Business has increased so they now have little carts. The carts make it feel more like a big grocery store and make it easier to shop.

Building your community doesn't take much. Until you try, you never know what you are missing. If you are not appreciating the little things that we sometimes ignore, you are missing a lot. All that is needed is to genuinely care, respect one another, and share life experiences to begin to experience community.

The pandemic kept us home bound, but it didn't stop us from existing and interacting with others. I am glad to see these new groups of essential workers being appreciated for their contribution to society.

Question

In a hundred years from now, will we still remember the essential workers of the COVID-19 pandemic; will we still realize the importance of workers who supply our basic needs?

The 1918, the Spanish Flu killed over 50 million people, among whom were many workers working on the front line, but there is no mention of this anywhere. I have checked and done extensive research, but most of the records and histories focus on how the virus spread and how many people died. There are also many references to the Red Cross and to nurses and doctors as the major front-line worker of the 1918 pandemic. The American Red Cross is made up of volunteers in many different fields, including food delivery, tailors who made masks during the pandemic, home aides who helped families fight the pandemic. Will this be the same story in a hundred years for the essential workers of COVID-19?

WE LIVE IN DIFFERENT TIMES FROM THE 1918 SPANISH FLU PANDEMIC – Today we have better resources for communicating than people had 100 years ago; resources that allow us to acknowledge the heroic efforts of essential workers who kept the economy running during the pandemic. Due to technological advances, we are more informed than the general public was during the 1918 pandemic. Access to news - TV, smart phones, and social media keep us abreast almost instantly. So, yes, there is a difference in how events of the Spanish Flu were recorded and how events of COVID-19 pandemic are recorded. Yes, everyone, and not just those in the media, can preserve the memories and heroic efforts of our brave essential frontline workers for the next generation. It is one of the core reasons for writing this book. It can provide information to readers fifty years from now.

Whatever avenue that you choose, continuing to acknowledge and appreciate the effort of essential workers for the next generation will make a huge difference. Here are some ideas that I have considered:

PHOTO ALBUM – making an album of favorite or profound moments featuring essential workers during the pandemic is one way to continue to spread and acknowledge the heroic work of our frontline workers. There are a lot of images out there. Our grandkids will thank us. If you don't have kids, you could donate your album to a local library or school.

VIDEO CLIPS – video is one of the major reasons why we know those that have come before us. Through documentaries and films this information has been preserved. Saving video clips of events that caught your attention and archiving them could benefit someone. You never know how far it could go.

START A FAMILY TRADITION OF KEEPING JOURNALS – Journals are a good way to record events. Passing one down through generations is a good way to preserve long gone events. Even a personal journal can be beneficial if it is made available to future generation.

Hopefully these suggestions will spark other ideas. There are many unique ways to share and preserve your personal experiences during the pandemic.

D. Jomo

Chapter Three
Honor & Help the
Elderly

Wrinkles should merely indicate where smiles have been.

Mark Twain

B y the end of March 2020, most news outlets and the CDC had declared immune compromised individuals and seniors to be at greater risk of having serious consequences if they got COVID-19. As the pandemic progressed the age group at highest risk was determined to be people 85 and older. As health officials realized that overall health and underlying conditions played a very important role, it became obvious that certain age groups were more susceptible to serious complications from the disease. These factors were important in not only determining who contracted the virus, but also in the severity of the symptoms. We also realized that more important than who contracted the virus was how severe the symptoms were as symptoms ranged from symptom-free to death.

When I learned of this, I reached out to a few seniors I knew to see how they were doing. Many were staying home and taking precautions. I offered to pick up groceries, if needed. A dear friend of mine who was 75, shared with me how she was mostly staying indoors and had congregants and friends help with errands. At 75 she was still very active, walking 3 miles a day and attending boxing classes. She would often say to me, "I don't feel 75 and you know what the secret is? Keep moving." I vividly remember her big smile as she said this to me with pride.

I couldn't help but wonder what this new life would do to her health if she stopped moving. Between the start of the pandemic and now, we lost three seniors in my building. I heard they died in their sleep. I was not aware if it was COVID related or not.

One day as I headed downstairs to my mailbox, I saw men moving things out of one of the apartments. A neighbor asked me if I wanted to look and see if there was something I liked or wanted. The deceased was in his 80s, I often met him in the elevator early in the morning on my way to work. He would go outside with his walker to pick up newspapers at the entrance to the building and bring them in the lobby.

I asked one of the movers why the man's relatives were not coming for his belongings? He told me that the only family he had was his brother—also in his 80s—who could not leave his home because of the pandemic. When I thought of all the seniors who were alone and unable to leave their homes, I was heart-broken and began looking around for ways to fill needs and programs that I could join to help the elderly. I was able to volunteer at a local food bank that delivered food to seniors' homes. In doing so, I realized more delivery programs for seniors were emerging to fill the gap created by the pandemic. This was exhilarating!

Outreach to Seniors Amidst the Pandemic

News reports of *meal delivery to the elderly* multiplied with the sudden awakening to the surge in need for food delivery to seniors. In April, a number of state governments launched new meal delivery programs. I was astounded by the fact that these programs did not exist in many areas before the pandemic! Although, I must admit that the need was not as great before the pandemic. I also realized that many areas had various meal delivery programs for seniors before the pandemic. By its nature, the pandemic resulted in seniors who were perfectly capable of caring for themselves, including shopping and preparing meals, who were now staying home to avoid coming into contact with someone who was contagious. This created a sudden demand for meal delivery that could not be met by the current services. I was heartened to see that services were being increased.

The living arrangement for most people change over their lifetime. As time progresses people go from living with family members to living with a spouse to living alone. As the number of elderly increases more elderly people are in the stage of living alone. Many eventually move to housing for the elderly. These range from independent living apartments to assisted or supportive living to nursing homes or hospitals. If you talk with seniors, you find a wide range of opinions on these various living options. Many seniors are fiercely independent, and resist attempts to curtail their independence in senior housing. The emotional ties to homes where they raised children or spent years with their spouses creates another barrier for finding housing that meets the needs of seniors on one hand. On the other, many seniors enjoy the social amenities and support offered in senior housing.

It seems to me that we tend to neglect the needs of the elderly, with so many seniors in need of services. We all go through the various stages of life, from infant to teenager, to young adult, to older adult, to senior. I highly commend those who created programs to help seniors during the pandemic. It was a good start. However, these are short-term solutions for a short-term problem. We can improve upon this foundation to create more sustainable programs for seniors for the long-term problems as the senior population increases.

QUESTION

While the pandemic escalated the need of many seniors, there are many issues that were not related to the pandemic. The pandemic just helped to point out the need for more services. How can we be more prepared to support seniors in the near future, knowing the elderly population is increasing?

BUILD HOMES THAT ARE SENIOR FRIENDLY – A very important fact is that many seniors wish to remain independent in the home they have lived in for years. A recent survey carried out by the US census bureau measuring whether US homes are ready for the aging population (projected to increase 16% by 2050) shows that only 10% of homes are designed to accommodate the aging in terms of wheel-chair accessibility and other support needs. While housing is driven by market desires, one thing to consider would be to support legislation that encourages senior friendly housing that does not interfere with what young home buyers are looking for or raise the price of housing for the young. For example, wider doorways to accommodate wheelchairs and wider stairs that can later accommodate chairlifts would not increase the price of housing significantly. Ranches are the best for seniors, but that is a little more difficult to accommodate economically as it can cause a major increase in pricing which is a big consideration for first time home buyers. This is especially true in cities and suburbs where land is expensive. Multi-story housing is cheaper to construct in terms of actual construction and land requirements. Maybe designers could focus on how multistory homes could be made accessible. For one thing, a closet could be located near stairways to accommodate elevators or lifts, if needed later.

Another idea is to help a senior citizen with simple improvements that can improve accessibility:

- Replace doorknobs with lever-type handles.
- Lower clothes rods. If you are handy, install a lower rod in the conventional way. If not, purchase the type that hangs from a higher rod. This is especially important for seniors that use wheelchairs or have other mobility issues.
- Research chairlifts and/or home elevators for a senior who cannot access the technology needed to do the research for themselves. Don't forget there is availability and a market for used chairlifts that are still in great shape. Also, look into places that provide financial assistance for these types of home improvements, if financial assistance is needed.
- Add a toilet riser with handles and/or replace the standard-height toilet with a taller model.
- Make sure electrical cords are out of the way.
- Repair chairs that are wobbly.

- Help move or discard items that clutter floor space. Rugs can increase the risk of falling for seniors.
- Check with the local town or senior center to see if a 'lending closet' is available for accessibility needs such as wheelchairs, toilet risers, etc. Offer to pick-up needed items or drive the senior to pick-up what is needed.

SOCIAL INCLUSIVITY - Learning and continuing social engagement are ways to retain healthy cognitive ability as we age. Some research shows that conversation is beneficial as it is one of the most demanding mental activities we engage in. Conversation requires a person to respond to ever changing stimuli. Staying mentally active helps delay the onset of issues associated with the decline in mental functioning. Imagine not being able to socialize and converse with others because of the lack of opportunities. While this might not be the case in many communities with large groups of seniors, we find there is often a lack of nearby activities for seniors in rural areas. Talking and communicating has been found to be one of the activities that are most helpful in maintaining cognitive ability.

ACTIONS PROMOTING SOCIAL INCLUSIVITY FOR SENIORS - Look at local senior centers to see what they offer. If you find the opportunities limited, think about what you could do. One thing is to facilitate a group. For example, Wednesday morning hobbies. You don't have to be able to do everything or anything. Just start a group where seniors can come to work on a project (knitting, scrapbooking, card making, drawing, anything really) while they socialize. This way, they can socialize with others while participating in an enjoyable activity. It is nonthreatening as new people don't have to worry about fitting in right away. They can work on their craft and slowly make friends. As the facilitator, you can keep people informed of meeting times and dates as well as being sure everyone has a ride. As time goes on, you could even solicit supplies for popular activities if there are seniors who are on a fixed income.

As individuals, we are morally obligated to look after the elders amongst us. The role of the elderly and how they are treated defines a culture and its people. Furthermore, most religious beliefs have something about the elderly embedded in their beliefs. Islam, Christianity, Judaism, and Hindu all emphasize honoring the elderly. The book of Zechariah found in both the Christian and Jewish Bibles calls for respecting elders. Whatever religion you profess, it is likely that you will find the directive to respect and honor your elders.

QUESTION

What can you do to promote and contribute to a culture that respects and provides for the elderly?

IDENTIFY NEEDS AROUND YOU – If you are like me, you are already wondering how you can make things different. Besides government organized initiatives you should be able to find small groups around you where your impact will be felt and appreciated. You could also organize or volunteer for local food drives. If you live in an apartment or condo, identify seniors in your building that need help. Offer to deliver groceries or drive them to doctor's appointments. Find ways to spend time with them and to engage in conversations. Just being a friend goes a long way in making another person feel valued and secure.

When I was a teenager, I used to be part of a group that visited senior homes every other weekend. One of the things that we did was spend time chatting with the seniors, asking how they were doing, asking about their loved ones, and their views on different topics. When we left, we would ask each senior we had a chat with if there was anything we could bring to them on our next visit.

I made friends with a 98-year-old woman, who had no living family. She was blind but after a few visits she could tell I was there when I walked into the room. I often brought her oranges as she loved them. This became a tradition. She would dress up on Saturday when I was coming and wait for me in her wheelchair. I would push her to the outdoor seating area where we would relax and chat until it was time for the group to leave.

After a few visits I realized there were other things I could do to help. Her wheelchair was difficult to push and uncomfortable to sit in. I was able to get her a new wheelchair by contacting the right department and letting them know that she was in need of a new one. I often did her laundry. So, I was able to identify clothing that she needed by paying attention to what was worn out and needed replacement. I requested a new mattress for her bed when I realized that hers was worn out. She felt like family, and we had an emotional attachment. I took the role of helping her seriously.

This was a small thing that did not require a lot of effort or money. No one ever heard about it, but it made a difference in her life and mine. It felt good seeing her all dressed waiting for me, knowing she was glad to see me, and loved my visits. Until you help someone else feel great about themselves, you might never know what it feels like when someone else's happiness is as a result of your actions. It is a great feeling no matter how small the action.

Seniors are an important part of our community and shouldn't be ignored. You can do your part by including them when possible and spending time with them when you can. Even a 20- or 30-minute conversation can make all the difference in the world to someone who is alone.

D. Jomo

Chapter Four
Individualism and Collectivism in a Pandemic

Coming together is a beginning. Keeping together is progress. Working together is success.

Henry Ford

One of my eureka moments as I watched news stories of events unfolding during the pandemic was the concept of individualism in our society and how much we rely on collectivist ideas. How could the two ideas work for society during a pandemic? Were they mutually exclusive or was there some middle ground? At first glance, it would seem that collectivism is superior to individualism, but if we look at other countries that have tried collectivism, we can see a number of problems. If we look at individualism in the extreme, with no thought of others we also see some issues that do not work well. While I am using these terms, I am not using them in the political sense. I found one definition of collectivism is the idea of land and production that is owned collectively (really by the government). This is not what I am referring to but rather the idea of concern for the group over a me first approach to life.

The right of an individual to choose to detach or exempt himself or herself from a collective goal is a key cornerstone in a free society. This can create problems during a pandemic if enough people ignore the common good. However, being individualistic does not mean the individual has no concern for the common good. In fact, it is only recently that the individual has considered their rights more important, even to the detriment of all others. We can clearly see this in the current military enlistment goals. Branches of the military are not able to find enough eligible candidates that are willing to serve in our current volunteer military.

As one general said, he believes the issue is a result of the fact that young men (this is not to exclude young women but most of our fighting force is comprised of men) no longer see military service as a sense of accomplishment, as something they would be proud of doing. It seems the responsibility to serve my country is no longer common or even taught to today's youth. In our evolving individualistic society, it is their right not to join the military when the country does not have a military draft in place. In a collective society, we would return to the draft as that would be necessary to meet the needs of the military and therefore, the common good. We also see this same problem with relationships which are not held in high esteem and family ties are not honored unless it benefits individual interest. This was not the norm of the past for individualism as family ties were strong and young men grew up with the concept of it being an honor to serve your country. However, today, even those with collectivist ideals are forsaking family over political and social goals. In the political sense, the collective society would find the common good would trump family ties and obligations, if there were a conflict.

What is the answer? As a group we need to return to the concepts of the past which honors both ideas. Remember, we are not talking about a form of government. We live in a free country where hard work and resourcefulness has resulted in creating a country where citizens are not limited to their station at birth. We need to continue this emphasis on personal effort to succeed while returning to the idea of community. In the past, it was not considered mutually exclusive to strive for individual success while helping those in need and serving your country. If we follow the Biblical command of working hard so that we have something to share with those in need, we will find a much better world. Individualism can work if we are not also absorbed in selfishness. We have to realize that making the world a better place for everyone makes it a better place for us. While those of the collective mindset need to realize, all need to be accountable to working hard if they are physically able.

Looking at the world today, collectivism seems like it could work, it could be the utopia we long for where everyone has enough, and no one is neglected. A google search reveals that collectivist societies value family relationships and the common good over individual wants. All this sounds great. However, if you continue reading you are directed to the works of Karl Marx and communism. The principles of political collectivism include more than just thinking of family and the common good. They include public ownership and government redistribution of wealth. The problem that collectivist societies run into is that incentive and motivation are stripped away from the individual while governmental corruption increases. What collectivist governments don't take into consideration is the abuse of power. In a collectivist (socialist/communist) society, government is all powerful because it has all the resources; it is redistributing the wealth and there is not enough to go around, especially with those in power having an unreasonably large share of the wealth. It also neglects human nature which runs towards selfishness whether in a collectivist or individualistic society. In an individualistic society, people are motivated to work hard for material gains which can be seen in a negative light as selfish. In a collectivist society people have no reason to work hard and can be seen in a negative light as lazy, which is the reason collectivist/communist societies struggle.

What is the answer? Returning to some of the good ideas of the past and incorporating some collectivist ideas into the individualist society. For example, teaching our children to care for others who are less fortunate. Finding ways to promote equal opportunities for all children to learn and become successful. I am reminded of the Chinese proverb: *Give a man a fish and you feed him for a day. Teach a man to fish and you feed him for a lifetime.* The idea is for the individual to help others in a sustainable way. This leaves the individual with the incentive to work hard while preventing government corruption and mismanagement of his wealth. The recipient is also motivated to work because he too will receive the benefits of his efforts rather than the shame of taking a handout when he is able to contribute to his success.

In the recent COVID pandemic we can see a problem with both orientations. When there is no commitment to collective action, some people will resist protocols. The collectivist will argue that it is not truly in the common good and the individualist will say they have a right—as an "individual"—to go unmasked and unvaccinated. We might all argue that there is no proven science behind these recommendations, or that individuals have the right to choose. But as we continue to see the deaths and the spread of the virus, a good response would be to work together to fight it. If the 'solutions' we have are not working, we need to work together to find solutions that do work. Working together against a common problem is not the same as a collectivist orientation. While this collective fight will be dear to the collectivist, most individualists also see the need to work together to solve a common problem. Indeed, working together to accomplish their goals has always been a strategy for the individual. Ridding the world of COVID is a goal that all can see as valuable.

In a collective society an individual identifies as part of a collective with goals and puts personal goals aside for the success of a collective goal. My proposal is not that an individualistic society has no benefit because having individual freedoms can only be achieved in an individualistic culture (Beyer 1968); but we need to balance it with the best collective concepts which integrate caring and building a cohesive society into our individual goals (Ellis 1996). As in the past, individualists who show care and concern for the needs of others will go a long way towards meeting goals that are good for everyone.

While I am aware of the good deeds many individuals do daily regardless of whether we are in a pandemic or not, I must say that I was amazed at the quick switch of the news to stories of individuals making a difference. Everything from making masks and distributing them as the country saw a shortage of masks to giving out hand sanitizers to shopping for shut ins. My hope is that when the pandemic is over, news outlets will still run stories of those who are making a positive contribution to society.

Some companies quickly converted their businesses to mask-making to fill the gap. Stores began implementing social distancing and requiring masks. At the start of the pandemic, I thought all I needed to do was stay home and take care of myself until it was over. But I wouldn't have made it this far without the effort of those people in my life who delivered groceries to me when I was sick and sent me masks that they made at home.

People who I had no personal relationships with went out of their way to constantly make sure that I was doing fine and had all I needed. I am sure we all experienced this in some way during the pandemic. And when I was able to give back, I volunteered at a food bank every week for the rest of the lockdown. I knew that people needed help and I wanted to help in some way. I was inspired by news stories of individuals not waiting on the government for action, and people finding ways to work with others. I had friends who drove three hours each day picking up food from the food bank to deliver to the homes of the elderly and the disabled. What I have learned is that people have the strength and capacity to step up in a crisis as they put aside their selfish tendencies whether they ascribe to the collectivist view or the individualist view.

THE ROLE OF NEWS STATIONS IN PROMOTING THE GOOD THINGS PEOPLE DO

News stations played a huge role in amplifying the efforts of individuals during the pandemic, it was as if all you saw on the news each time you tuned in was a story of an individual or group helping those in need. Although many of these activities had existed before the pandemic, most went unnoticed and were not deemed newsworthy. As the news broadcasted the best efforts of the American people, others were inspired to step up and contribute in ways they had not previously considered.

I must also say that the reason for my fascination and pointing out these good deeds is the difference in the number of good deeds I was aware of during the pandemic compared to before the pandemic. While I know some things existed previously, I was totally unaware of most of them. So, I understand if this does not apply to you, or you are not as fascinated as I am because you were already helping others and aware of the good deeds going on in your community before the pandemic. I believe there were two reasons that I was unaware of what was happening. First, the number of things happening was increasing as people stepped up to meet the needs of the crisis. Second, news stations were publicizing these good deeds so that more people became aware of what was going on.

Pandemic or not, I have always been one that believed in contributing to my community no matter how small. So, I was a part of a knitting group that knitted hats, sweaters, gloves, etc. for a jail ministry (I haven't been active in this group for a while). I was an active food bank volunteer as I volunteered to cook hot meals for the homeless. I volunteered for anything that I could that benefited my community.

After the second week of the pandemic, I noticed an increase in the number of volunteers in some groups that I volunteered with. For example, one group with a large increase in volunteers was the food bank. The increase in help was obvious as we cut our preparation time by about a third. We usually started at 8 AM and finished packing for first set of home deliveries at 11 AM. Suddenly, every bag was packed and ready to go out the door before 10. This was because more people were volunteering. I often chatted with people who shared that they had not volunteered before now and they felt called during this time to do something to help. As a result, the load was lightened for all, and we were finishing early.

QUESTION

How do we create a more caring individualistic mindset? What can we do so that we are aware of and respond to the needs in our community while working hard to pursue personal goals?

I and WE

I started by thinking about using the term *I* vs. *we*. It is a good way to recognize whether you are thinking of others or just yourself. You will find that sometimes, the 'I' focus is the most appropriate – I'm wearing my blue shirt today or I'm visiting my mom today. On the other hand, using "we" in a statement indicates an awareness of community whether the team at work, the neighbors in your building, or the people in world. Everyone should have some plans to help those who are less fortunate. How and when you do that will depend on your personal situation and your passions but the use of the term 'we' can help you to focus on who and where help is needed.

For example, in New York volunteers gathered at City Harvest to pack and deliver food to those in need. In Wroclaw, Poland, volunteers delivered coffee, energy drinks, water, and sack lunches to doctors and nurses working overtime. Many contributed to crowd-funding campaigns for people who were out of work and couldn't afford meals. Some walked dogs for the elderly who were unable to get out.

In Australia, the owner of Glee Bookstore used a free bicycle service to send books to people at home. In Afghanistan, a young lady named Basira Popul organized a team to deliver bars of soaps to homes so people could wash their hands to reduce the spread of the virus.

How many times have you used the word "I" today? Could you have replaced it with "we"? If yes, think about the difference that might make.

Individuals and government organizations must also understand when to use "I" vs. "we." In New Zealand, for example, the 'we" statement brought about the feeling of accountability and team effort. I don't know about you, but if I'm working with a team where the leader constantly uses the "I" statement and only refers to his/her accomplishments, I am more likely to be lackadaisical, compared to a leader who constantly reminds us that "we" are a team seeking a common goal.

I believe "we" have in our hands the power to fight this virus and beat the pandemic by making informed decisions, by looking at the numbers, and research. We have the power to work together to make the world a better place once the pandemic is history. We came together offering help to the vulnerable at the start of the pandemic. We must stay committed to one another and maintain the unity we developed at the start of the pandemic and on into the future.

I considered a few ideas to make an effort to start with our community. A few things could be done differently in terms of taking a step:

First, differentiate which needs are the most important and need the most effort and support to accomplish and which needs can wait or will have to wait due to lack of resources.

Secondly, after identifying needs and their importance level, make a list of what needs to be done to address those needs in the order of importance and availability of resources.

Thirdly, see what resources are available to you in terms of funds, supplies, time, etc. This may change the order of your list.

Lastly, take proactive steps. Remember, start with small steps and trust the process to get things changed. See what you can do without help. Follow with ideas that need a group effort. If an identified need requires a change in the law, is there someone in your network that can help push the change forward? Be intentional in your actions to make an impact by considering the impact of your choices and decisions on those around you.

Chapter Five
The Underserved

It is one of the most beautiful compensations of life that no man can sincerely try to help another without helping himself.

Ralph Waldo Emerson

The Oxford dictionary defines underserved as "an area or group of people not getting enough help, products, or services." As COVID-19 death cases increased, underserved populations seemed to bear the brunt of the illness. There are many speculations as to why this is true, but we will not address those here except as how to help those groups.

I mentioned in the previous chapter that this book will give account of events that light up the beam of hope during the pandemic and also provide solutions from my point of view. Nonetheless, the truth is that in order to understand the present and to measure progress we must look back to history and similar events that were handled differently. It is not to say that we still live in such society, but to emphasis progress and possible solutions to possible eradiation of the said problem. How communities, race, and ethnic groups were viewed in connection to today. While I discuss the underserved in both past and present tense, it is my hope, to invoke a perception of hope and possibilities around us.

In light of the current situation in the world, we see U.S. news stories of which communities are hit hardest by the pandemic. African Americans, Latinos, Native Americans, and some Pacific Island communities faced difficulties in navigating services as the country sheltered in place.

In 2020, the Center for Disease Control and Prevention (CDC) reported that these groups had been the hardest hit. According to a study (*COVID-19 Deaths in the Ten Across Region*, 2021), conducted by American Public Media using CDC's data, reported that despite the COVID-19 virus having no "known biological reason to predispose a particular ethnic group or race," there is a huge gap in how each race and ethnic group access care, putting the world at a risk of staying in the pandemic longer than it should. Availability of services had a wide range of variation depending on the location of those needing services. Those in rural areas had less access to health care but they also had less exposure to others. Another issue would be cultural that resulted in some families continuing to engage in large family activities which increased the risk of contracting the virus. I know some would say this makes it their own fault but engaging in large family get-togethers is often a cultural norm. The idea that needs to be considered is how can these family gatherings be safer for the participants.

Another research report (*Black Communities Are Hit Hardest By COVID-19 in Louisiana and Elsewhere*, 2021) showed that black Americans living in Louisiana and Mississippi experienced the highest death rates. By the end of March 2020, the Louisiana Department of Health reported that "more than 70 percent of residents who died from COVID-19 were black." These figures are very concerning. While Louisiana has one of the highest populations of people of color, blacks represent just under 35% of the population. As a nation, we need to research the reason why they experienced 70% of the deaths. While lack of health care may well be the reason, we are not helping anyone if we just jump on that bandwagon. With less than 40% of the population black, the death rate is significant and deserves a closer look, if we are to find solutions.

The numbers indicate the same trend in cities like Chicago with just over 30% of the population black (about 4% different from Louisiana) they reported between 60 and 70 percent of the deaths were also from black communities. This would seem to negate rural communities as the cause. A report by Tegan Wendland on WWNO – New Orleans Public Radio reported how difficult it was to get the number of death rates by race from the department of health.

One thought is that in lower income groups (about 27 percent) live in crowded multi-generational households as a result of poverty, making it difficult to social distance from other family members. About 15.1 percent of high-risk blacks lived in households with at least one worker in the health sector versus 9.3 percent of whites. About 56.5 percent of blacks lived in households with at least one worker who was unable to work from home. This is true for low-income families regardless of race, but a larger percentage of the total black population is low-income than the percentage of whites. Another thought is that strong family ties result in larger and more frequent family get-togethers. It has also been suggested that lower income families are less likely to seek medical attention until the symptoms are severe. This would result in mild cases not being reported or not even being known, thereby effecting the statistics. This also could have resulted in people not seeking treatment until it was too late, increasing the rate of mortality.

During the Spanish Flu, some thought that some minority groups were biologically inferior and thus more susceptible to infection and diseases. W.E.B. Du Bois (1906) argued that "with improved sanitary conditions, improved education, and better economic opportunities," the health of African Americans would improve. I believe this could be true today and is likely to be a contributing factor in Coronavirus for all demographics of those with low income.

Unfortunately, these are not quick fixes. Let's take improved education. That needs to start in kindergarten or even before, taking years to see the improved results. In many low-income areas 8th-grade students are already so far behind, it is impossible to catch up with the interventions available today. Not to mention, the number of students that struggle with grade level instruction in low-income neighborhoods make it financially impossible to provide needed interventions from the current school budget. Better economic opportunity has been directly related to education. Again, bringing out the fact that the problem is not a quick fix. Those in higher-income districts do not have as many students struggling. Therefore, the cost of providing interventions to struggling students is less because the number of students in need is less.

One proposed solution for better opportunities is equity grading. While that sounds good on the surface, if we look at it more closely, it is just a cost-effective way that eliminates the need to provide better education while appearing to be helpful. What it really boils down to is simply giving marginalized students the same grade as other students without regard to what was actually learned. For example, if a marginalized student earned a C with a 75%, the teacher would give him or her an A because the students had fewer opportunities to learn. While that may sound right, the goal of education is not good grades. The goal of education is to educate students. Giving that student an A does nothing to educate him or her. Nor does it help provide opportunities that are based on a good education.

Take just a minute and see how grade equity plays out for the student. The two students (let's call them John and William) both enroll in the next math class which is required to graduate. When we check in on them, we see William who earned an A with 95%, is doing great. John on the other hand is struggling and has been talking to the counselor about dropping the class. The reason he is struggling is because even though he had an A, he was not taught all the things he needed to know to be successful in the next math class. When John drops the class, he is eliminating better opportunities that he would enjoy if he were able to graduate from college. Remember, the key to any solution for education has to result in students actually learning.

On July 19, 2022, *The Color of Coronavirus* was updated. With the new statistics, Asians have had the highest percentage of increase (based on May 2022 statistics) of reports of Coronavirus, with a 49% increase. Whites had a 20% increase with black and Hispanics having no increase. If we look overall, Native Americans have been the hardest hit with 459 deaths per 100,000. Even with the large increase for Asians, they are still in the lowest range with 164 deaths per 100,000 followed by Hispanics with 264 per 100,000. Interestingly enough, the whites with 334 and the blacks with 348 per 100,000 were the closest. (When calculated 'per 100,000' we eliminate the need to calculate based on percentage of the population.) The data was not in-depth enough to determine if the change is the result of better data. Possibly, the black and Hispanic communities reached herd immunity sooner with a high value on family and larger family get-togethers and intergenerational homes. While the data isn't as readily available, some research has shown that hospitalization and morbidity is higher for low-income persons regardless of race or ethnicity. Perhaps this is due to low-income patients not seeking care until they have serious symptoms. Perhaps it is due to lesser availability of preventative care and early care to lessen symptoms and duration of illness. Perhaps it is due to the financial cost involved in seeking health care and getting to the appointment.

Another interesting fact, research carried out by authors from the University of Pennsylvania found a huge gap in mortality rates between whites living in rural areas vs those in urban areas (not just for COVID), "the data show that white men in large central metropolitan areas had the biggest gains in life expectancy; the Middle Atlantic and Pacific regions gained 7.13 and 6.11 years over the study period, respectively. By contrast, white men in nonmetro areas of Appalachia, and the East and South-Central states—Alabama, Mississippi, Tennessee, Kentucky, Arkansas, Louisiana, Texas, and Oklahoma—saw gains of 1.42 to 1.80 years" (Caffrey, 2019). What is the cause – lack of healthcare resources? Lack of education? Lack of confidence in healthcare that results in not accessing what is available? These are all difficult questions, but the idea is that we should be considering them as that will give us an idea of where to start to solve the problem.

QUESTIONS

- What role does the availability of health care play in these statistics?
-
- Does the reliance on and choice of healthcare options make a difference?

- Do food choices and/or availability of food have a role?

- Does the data imply a racial issue or socio-economic reason? How would this change the possible solutions to the problem?

I am sure by now you know where I am going with this. This is everyone's problem. If there is one thing the pandemic has taught me, it is that we are more alike than I realized. Within the short period of 18 months, the virus has killed about 4.8 million people worldwide, caused many to be unemployed, and destroyed businesses without consideration of race or ethnic group. Coronavirus is no respecter of persons. We must fix underlying problems affecting the underserved communities because it is the right thing to do. I believe education and equal opportunity are the only sustainable solutions. While we may need some short-term solutions, the sooner we start with education, the sooner many problems will begin to be erased.

We are all connected. The Bible makes this emphasis in the book of Galatians, "There is neither Jew nor Gentile, neither slave nor free, nor is there male and female, for you are all one in Christ." In a country founded on the grounds of Christian morality, I hope we can make this the norm as we choose to "love our neighbors as ourselves."

QUESTION

What needs to change?

START WITH YOU! In the past couple of years since the "Me too" movement was brought to our attention (2017) I have frequently heard the statement "silence is complacency", and I strongly agree. I am not vocal and avoid getting into arguments in response to matters of race and inequality, simply because I choose to focus on finding solutions rather than argue. But I believe we all have a voice and should stand for something. At the end of the day, it is your actions that count rather than your thoughts. Having a voice doesn't necessarily mean standing on the corner of the street protesting or starting a movement. We are not all built that way, nor do we all have the opportunity or platform to do so. However, we can all do something to start the process. While the Me Too movement was important, we can't forget the need to think of others.

QUESTION

What are you good at?

FOCUS ON YOUR STRENGHTS! If you are not already doing something to help those less fortunate than yourself, look for something you can do. Find one thing you are good at and one place you can make a difference. If that does not work for you, try something else. There are many opportunities to help others. It is often not the quantity that matters but the quality of your action.

QUESTION

Are you part of a small group?

SHARE YOUR IDEAS ABOUT PROBLEMS IN YOUR COMMUNITY WITH YOUR SMALL GROUP! Your small group is the best place to start. It might be just your family or friends. I once had an acquaintance tell me about her struggles with her grandfather and some relatives who still had a hard time accepting people from minority groups like African Americans as equals or as humans with equal human rights. I have known her for quite some time but never knew this about her family. Changing her family's perspective was a cause that she had silently taken upon herself. Like her, your idea of making a difference might not make the headlines.

Maybe you could identify barriers in the community that are stopping people in your community from accessing benefits or opportunities. Like helping a non-English speaker in your small group or neighborhood fill out an application. Or identifying opportunities in the community that they may benefit from and pointing out the opportunities. For example, during the pandemic, there were a few grants and loans to help families/businesses pay rent, but many were not aware of those grants. Inform your small group and offer help to anyone who needs help with applying.

CHOOSE YOUR BATTLES! There is a saying that goes "choose your battles wisely." I don't know about you, but I go into battle with the sole purpose of winning and thus, it often seems like I spend too much time discussing issues before I take action to help someone. Just to make sure I'm all in, I carry out risk assessment and look for other possible solutions. Rather than arguing philosophy, I look for specific ways to help others. What I have found is that many times, when arguing, my point of view is really not as different as someone else's. In reality, we are saying the same thing differently. At times, it is a matter of emphasis. For example, I may emphasize helping the elderly while someone else is focused on young people. Neither of us are wrong, we just have different talents or see the greatest need differently. Other times, it is all about word choice – language is loaded with a lot of preconceived ideas. What creates a negative connotation to one person may not be the message another is trying to share (think back to the terms individualist and the collectivist which are often interpreted in a political context that I did not intend).

BE INFORMED ABOUT EVENTS AROUND YOU! It is in *knowing* that you can help change things for the better. Be informed, understand your community, what it needs the most, and work on filling the gap, taking one step at a time.

"A fight for one is a fight for all" – **WHY WE MUST NOT LEAVE ANYONE/COUNTRY BEHIND**

The U.S, imports more goods than it exports. "In 2019, the total U.S. trade with foreign countries was $5.6 trillion. That was $2.5 trillion in exports and $3.1 trillion in imports of both goods and services." (Office of the United States Trade Representative)

Neglect of underserved communities and countries could be devastating. It will also interrupt free flow of trade and movement for businesses from one country or the other if COVID-19 cases rise.

Consider the value imports from some African countries. In 2019, the United States imports from Kenya totaled $667 million. U.S. total imports of agricultural products from Kenya totaled $126 million in 2019. Leading categories include tree nuts, coffee, tea, essential oils, and vegetable oils.

The U.S. imports from Nigeria in 2019 totaled $4.6 billion. U.S. total imports of agricultural products from Nigeria totaled $50 million in 2019. Leading categories include cocoa beans, feed, tea, spices, and tree nuts. These might seem like small numbers but imports from all over the world no matter how small help countries by providing much needed income.

As the United States prepares to reopen and reduce its COVID orders, India is dealing with a rise in COVID cases with only 3.6% of its population vaccinated. A BBC news report on May 24, reported a 7-day average death rate of 4000. The problem in India is not only the shortage of vaccine but also lack of hospital beds for those infected. Several images of people lying on the streets of India and outside hospitals already filled to full capacity were all over the news.

D. Jomo

QUESTION

What do you see around you that doesn't seem right? When I am in the city, I see many homeless people. What is the homeless situation like in your area? Can we support the programs in our city to help the homeless?

One thing I do to help the homeless in my community is listen to them and make them feel seen and heard. For example, one afternoon in 2016, I stopped at Ghirardelli, the famous San Francisco chocolate shop to grab chocolate cookies (in my opinion, still the best warm cookie around). At the park, I asked a well-dressed man in his 60's if I could sit and chat with him. I didn't know him, but I saw him there every day, sitting on the same corner of the street. People often handed him spare change and food as they hurried passed on their way to their destinations. Our long conversation on various topics included his advice to invest in penny stocks and asking me to help him type a letter he had written to the mayor for a program he wanted to run in the Tenderloin district. I got to know that he was a Vietnam War Veteran and was homeless but still found a way to dress up and sit there every day to pass time. At night he would look for a nearby shed or doorway to sleep. We talked for over 30 minutes, and I promised to type his letter to the mayor. I offered to put $5 in his plate (where people drop change as they walk by) but he declined insisting that I needed it more since I was a student. I had previously mentioned to him about a class I was taking at the time. "Keep it kid, you need it more than me. You're still a student," he said. Then we exchanged phone numbers.

A few months later, he was gone from that corner. His phone was not reachable, and I got really worried. Finally, almost six months later, I heard someone call out my name from down the block, "Dee, Dee, Dee." I turned and it was him. I was so happy to see him well and alive that I hugged him. I asked his whereabouts for the last few months and found he had gotten an SRO (single room occupancy) and was beginning a project somewhere in the community. He thanked me for talking to him, picking up his calls when he called, and believing in him enough to sit with him on the street and chat.

What he didn't understand was that he helped me even more by the life hacks and advice he gave to me in those chats. Lessons learned and things he would do differently if given a second chance were also helpful to me. So, while there is no one way or no manual on how to help the homeless, use your initiative to understand your environment, be observant of what's happening around you, think of the best way to approach the situation in a way that works for you.

We could argue that this was a special case of a homeless man who had clarity and vision. We might ask, what about homeless people with mental health issues, drug addiction, or drinking problems who cannot engage in a meaningful conversation? At the end of the book, I list several resources and organizations that advocate for the homeless with mental health issues, hopefully you can find one like that around your environs to be a part of or recommend to individuals that need it.

Before I became aware of such programs, I used to think that homeless individuals with mental health issues were a lost cause and unapproachable as well, mostly in fear for my safety. But the truth is that for many of these individuals, our support and the right resources can often start them on a journey to recovery. The conversation needs to be had about what can be done. What sustainable options are available and what short-term options are needed?

In 2015, an organization in New York, Brooklyn Community Housing and Services (BCHS) helped 97 homeless individuals who were suffering from different mental health issues get housing. A year later 97% of them still maintained their housing or were able to move into better housing after gaining income to support living outside the program. This may seem pointless as some statistics state there are over half a million homeless individuals in the U.S. The big idea is that the recidivism is only 3% and it is a place to start. This gives us an idea of what works and that this is a program that should be expanded.

The organization credits it's success to a foundation of treating these individuals with respect, providing health care (nurses), and case workers who helped them navigate the system individually for as long as it took them to get back on their feet. The clients were accepted as they were, with understanding for each individual's needs and designing a specialized plan to manage the individual challenges faced by participants rather than a generalized program that doesn't work for everyone.

Lastly, listen to your inner self. Help as you are called and led. There are many ways you can help; you just have to find what works for you.

QUESTION

How about the long-term sustainability? Do you have any ideas? If you do find ways that work, share your ideas with your circle. Word travels!

In addition to providing nursing care and housing support, The Brooklyn Community Housing and Services (BCHS) also provides training and recovery orientation to further support the homeless they work with. Educating the homeless on the need to remain in the program and its benefits is one way to promote sustainability and help individuals stay in the program longer as they learn new skills and ways to navigate the world once they are back on their feet.

Learning helps each and every one of us understand why we do what we do, and its benefits to our life and health. Designing more programs to educate the homeless will sensitize them about certain dangers and why they should embrace change.

D. Jomo

Chapter Six
A Broken World –
Social Justice &
Equality

Finding beauty in a broken world is creating beauty in the world we find.
Terry Tempest Williams

I mentioned earlier that this book was written to highlight events of hope amidst the pandemic with an emphasis on my observations and thoughts. The events on TV showcased the fact that we do not live in a perfect world. Amidst stories of heroic acts were complaints, violence, and social unrest.

Many were fighting in the name of social justice and equality while others took advantage of the situation to burn, loot, and destroy. In doing so, they were destroying their own community as well as the larger community. It is important that everyone help in the fight to eradicate injustice in all its forms. However, there is a lot of disagreement over what that means exactly, and which solutions should be instituted. For my purpose, I am thinking of the idea that everyone should have an equal opportunity to succeed. Further, it is important that we look at issues honestly without just jumping on a bandwagon that sounds good. In doing so we will not solve problems and are likely to make them worse.

QUESTION

What do others say about us and the role we play in making this a better world for everyone? What will history have to say about us? What will it say about our generation? Our church? Our community? Our country?

I am constantly thinking of the world that I will leave behind after I'm long gone. We must not forget the delicateness of life and the inevitable nature of death that awaits us all. As I wake up every morning, I now cherish the blessing that is life itself and remind myself of how lucky I am to be alive and breathing the air. Even so, as I count my blessings, I see nations rise against nations. Consider history: conquests by the Roman Empire, the Crusades in the Middle East, forceful colonialization of African and Asian continents, world wars, the Cold War, and the Jewish Holocaust to name a few. During these atrocities, time stopped for the victims, they lived with the inflicted wounds for years and with the pain and suffering caused by others. Events such as the detonating of nuclear bombs in Hiroshima in 1945 that left its citizens physically and biologically deformed, the mass killing of Jews in the gas chambers in the 1930's, the Atlantic slave trade where Africans were stacked like commodities in boats to the Western world, and the lynching of African Americans in the South are some of the major blackmarks on humanity. Even on a lesser scale, how much psychological damage is caused by treating a fellow human with disrespect and complete disregard of their equality. Just look at our schools and the emotional trauma experienced by students as a result of rampant bullying that is going largely unchecked. These scars remain for the individual, but the world moves on without solving the underlying problem.

Then I considered economic inequality which is sometimes referred to as the umbrella for which all other inequality problems are classified. It seems, based on research that COVID definitely impacted the poor more than those who were well off. What is the answer? During the pandemic we saw that many of the upper and middle class were able to stay home to keep their family safe, those that had jobs mostly worked from home unless they worked in health care and yet the wealthy continue to get wealthier (*Global Inequality*, 2021).

QUESTION

What if we provide equal education and opportunities for all, so everyone has the opportunity to get the same level of education? Horace Mann said, "Education is the great equalizer." If we look at longitudinal studies of children living in poverty, white or black, we find that the students who are successful adults are most often the ones who got an education. What can be done to increase the number of children that get a good education? How do we educate children who do not value education? What needs to be done to get 'buy-in' from these students so that they are engaged in the educational process? How do we educate parents who do not value education as this is passed on to their children? We know it can be done; the outliers have demonstrated the fact that it is possible. All children can succeed. How do we make it happen?

THE ROLE YOU PLAY - There is much brokenness to repair. It begins with educational opportunities. It is not a quick fix, but it is sustainable. If we look back through history, we will see that change doesn't happen by simply accepting what is. We need to take education out of the political arena and see what actually works. Currently, it is politically incorrect to say that what works for middle class suburban kids will not work for low-income students – black or white or brown. So, what do we do as a result of this faulty premise due to political correctness? Currently, we take programs and methods that are successful in upper- and middle-class schools and use them to attempt to help students in Title 1 (low-income) schools. Then we are surprised when it doesn't work because we believe the kids have the same needs. While the intentions were good, the results are not because they are based on the faulty premise that the needs of the students are the same.

Instead, we need to look at the few examples of what is working in low-income schools because the needs of low-income students are different than the needs of middle- and upper-income students. While it is technically true that the students are the same, it is the needs that should guide the process. If we can't find enough low-income schools that are successful, look for individual teachers in those schools. There are teachers that are successful, there are even movies made about some of these teachers. Let's look to see what they are doing. Saying that the needs of low-income students are different is not a bad thing. It does not speak to the potential of the student. It does not reflect on the innate ability of the student. Low-income students are just as capable of success if we can get rid of the politics and meet the needs of the students.

PEACEFUL APPROACH - Although we still fight to achieve what Martin Luther King Jr. and the Freedom Riders constantly fought for, we must give credit to the powerful effect of the peaceful tactic of the civil rights movements of the 1960's and adopt such peaceful tactics in finding common ground and solutions to our problems. But we must do it together—each race, ethnic group, and nationality—to create change because it affects us all. We have come a long way since the days of Dr. King's famous speech, but we still have a way to go. Continue to press forward peacefully until the problem is solved.

A good example of a peaceful approach would be sending a proposal to your representative asking for a community center to give underprivileged youth a safe outlet for social activities. Or better yet, see what government buildings already exist that could be used for after school activities. If we could spend half of the time we spend pointing out problems to find solutions we would all be making positive changes around us no matter how small. If low-income areas near you already have a community center, look into the programs and activities offered there. A safe place is important. So are supervised activities, help with homework, structured sports activities, mentoring programs, and classes on resumes and career choices for older students.

Question

So, what prevents us from having equal opportunity for all? What steps can be taken to move toward that goal?

In a paper titled "Birds of a Feather: Homophily in Social Networks," Miller McPherson writes on the importance of expanding your social circle to include people of other races and ethnicities, explaining that, "when you are only interacting with people like yourself, it causes you to form inaccurate beliefs about other people."

A COMMUNITY FOR ALL - I do not personally believe in the superiority of one being over the another. However, we are shaped by our experiences. Our communities, schools, friends, and leaders shape who we are making each of us a unique individual. So, we must create a welcoming community for all where people are treated equally. Children raised in neighborhoods and communities that lack basic infrastructures are no different from those who live in luxury. However, the needs of every child is different whether we are talking rich or poor, white or black, loved or unloved.

We should not measure one child against another in regard to potential or worthiness. As our American Constitution states, all men are created equal. This is not to say we are all the same, but we all have the same value. We are all entitled to opportunity. One person is not worth more than another based on their station in life, their race, their income, or any other way that we classify people. Nor does this mean that we have had it right since that document was penned. The document is the ideal that we should be striving to reach. Fortunately, we have progressed past the time when the state of the Union literally meant, 'all white **men**' excluding women and all blacks, male or female. Have we reached perfection? No, but we have come too far on the journey to stop now. What are the next steps to continue that journey? Where do we see inequality? Where do we see opportunity based on race? Where do we see employment and income based on gender?

* * Question* *

How do we repair the brokenness in our world and open dialogue to create a more just world? How do we create equal opportunities?

CREATING EQUAL OPPORTUNITY - Ultimately, individual people must solve this problem. While the government creates policies and controls the judicial system, they do not tell you how to live your lives daily. It is our moral obligation to make sure we leave a peaceful world for the next generation. It is easy for us to blame the system and the government. I'll again go back to education. There can be no equal opportunity without a quality education for all. The best paying jobs go to those who are the best educated because they will make the most money for the company. Occasionally, we see someone without education rising through the ranks as those higher up see an innate ability in someone who lacks a formal education, but this isn't the rule. Sometimes, someone like Bill Gates comes along who is essentially a dropout billionaire, but how many more can you name in that category? So, when we talk equal opportunity, we have to think in terms of children, not adults. If we think of adults, then we are trying to solve the symptom – adults who do not receive an education are unable to compete in today's job market. The skills they have to offer an employer are not worth as much money as the skills an educated person has to offer the company. We must make sure students are gaining the skills that allow them to compete in the adult world on an equal footing, skills that will allow them to make significant contributions at their place of employment and to the world.

Question

Who is the government? Who created the system?

Individuals like you and I created the system and men and women that we elect run the government. If the system was created by us, it can be changed in the same way by us. We can recommend laws that bring about change in our constituencies. We must create a world for all to gain access to education, health care, technology, and job opportunity. We must find ways to treat each other with love and respect. A safe and peaceful world free of hate, crime, and discrimination is only possible as we get to know one another.

NON-GOVERNMENT INITIATIVE – Before the pandemic I often associated a huge part of social justice and inequality problem with lack of government efforts in ensuring equal infrastructure made available in all states. For example, if my street is not clean, I put the blame on my district representative not paying attention to the area that I live, my part of the country. Unfortunately, we sometimes have the notion that our elected official was elected to solve the problem and if you're not in office, it is not your responsibility.

The truth is we can't wait on the government to solve all the problems. I have in previous chapters emphasized the need to take personal actions. Yes, we can argue that it is the government's responsibility or that the wealthy should do more, but the only person we control is ourselves. We need to ask, is there something I can do?

Some non-government initiatives include:

- Locate a non-profit in your community to contribute your skills and ideas about filling inequality gaps in your community. Many non-profit organizations seek members for their board of directors with aligned visions and goals to lead. If you have the capacity to fill that role, consider applying for a board member position to an organization you are passionate about. As a board member you will be helping to make decisions and shape policy.
- Volunteer – community centers and places like veteran's homes, senior homes, food banks, etc. can often use help and need donations to continue providing services. Find an organization that helps in an area that aligns with your passions and volunteer or provide funds to support the organization.
- Mentorship – there are many organizations that have mentorship positions to help children. (Note that these usually require a background check and training to keep children safe). See what is available in your area. Start with a short-term commitment and if it works well, increase your level of support.
- Parenting – the job of parenting is not limited to adults with biological children. You could become a foster parent and provide a home for displaced children in your community. (Note that becoming a foster parent is not about you, it is about helping children. You will need training, a home study, a

background check, and the personality to love difficult children who are hurting.) If you enjoy children, this could be an area for you. If you work well with teens and enjoy spending time with them, teens are especially hard to place. Keep in mind that all children in foster care have experienced trauma, some more than others. As a result, many have difficulty regulating their emotions. If you are able to love a child that is struggling while helping them understand and control their emotions, this would be a perfect opportunity for you to share your abilities.

- Donate to your local school. If you live in an area where the school has plenty of money, consider donating to a low-income school. It could be money or an old family piano sitting in your basement that could be put it to use. Many public schools are also in need of orchestra and band instruments for students who cannot afford to purchase or rent an instrument. Some high schools are even in need of used cars for their automotive repair programs. Remember, if your local school does not need these items, check with a school in a low-income area.

Some of these ideas you may already know about or participate in. These are just a few proposals that you can take personally, but there are many more out there. Just look around you.

GLOBAL PERSPECTIVE – Keep in mind that we are first humans and people with common goals. Avoidance of categorizing or defining ourselves by country and nation is one way to move forward. While pride in your heritage or country is not a problem, do not use it to exclude others in the world. Our actions in our respective countries affect individuals in other countries.

My perspective of the world in terms of globalization before the pandemic was that we are constantly competing in every aspect of our economy, including education and resources. The idea of wealth defining how much power a country possesses has always been the way that I viewed the world. But the pandemic has changed that ideology for me. I am now trying to think globally and how to improve the situation of our world, not just my country or my city.

D. Jomo

Chapter 7
Time to Change
Focus

The ultimate measure of a person is not where one stands in moments of comfort and convenience, but where one stands in times of challenge and controversy.
Martin Luther King, Jr

Time to Change Focus

It seems to me that we have long focused on the direction of creating change among the older demographic and paying less attention to addressing grassroot causes of how this problem is passed from one generation to another. Just as equal opportunity has to start with a good education for all, nurturing children to live with respect and concern for their fellow man has to start early, before children begin school. Perhaps if we look at parents who are doing this well, we can understand what it takes to parent a child well, to improve the future for coming generations.

Despite arguments that as we grow older, we pick up new habits (good/bad), research shows that unlearning old habits to learn new ones is often difficult. The time and effort required to successfully unlearn something lessens the success rate for learning new habits. Thus, the saying "old habits die hard." The famous song, "You've Got to be Carefully Taught," from *South Pacific*, "before you are six, or seven, or eight," sums it up well. While the song talks about how young children are taught to hate, the opposite, teaching children to love and respect, is also true.

I remember a friend's daughter coming back from school at three years old and describing her new friends in school as "peach" and "tanned peach." In trying to understand why she made the distinction we realized that one child was Caucasian, and the other was Asian. We asked what color she was, and she said "I am brown" while motioning to the color pallet on the table. She wasn't seeing through the same lens that we view the world but from that which her teacher had taught her, the color pallets for her coloring book. When we speak of skin color, we are not speaking of an actual color as the child was but rather a label that has been assigned to that color of skin.

Today at ten years old she knows the difference between a black child and a white child. She knows that peach and tan peach exist only in her crayon box. I tease her every now and then asking if she remembers referring to her friends as peach and tan peach and she has no recollection of it, but rather quickly corrects me with her view of them now. Even though her mom never sat her down to make these distinctions, she has been shaped by her environment and learned the social usage of skin color from her friends and family. While this example is not negative, it is meant to show that children learn from their environment.

Question

What is it about our environment that influences this change as we get older? What role does the media play? What role does our immediate environment play?

IDENTIFY ENVIROMENTAL PROVOCATIONS -

Although most children under the age of three cannot express themselves as skillfully as an adult most of the time, they observe the environment that they live in. They know when they are in an environment different from what they are accustomed to and often identify with the environment they are used to as the only option or better than any other option. This is the beginning of the child learning to see the bigger world, having moved developmentally from an awareness of self to family to neighborhood. The child will continue to become aware of an ever-widening circle until he or she develops a global perspective. The family and social group will influence this developing global awareness.

Growing up, my dad was into cars. He moved with the trend and often had whatever car was trending. So, my brothers automatically fell in love with cars. Although I wasn't particularly intrigued by cars, I enjoyed sitting in the front seat and listening to them argue as they claimed ownership of the cars we drove by on our way to school. "That's my car." "No, I said it first, it's my car."

With time this progressed into guessing names of the cars we drove by on our way to school. In both instances I noticed how they skipped cars that weren't in good condition, cars that had been in accidents, that didn't look flashy in appearance, or that weren't expensive, like

Mercedes, Volvos, Jeeps, BMWs, convertibles, etc. Those were cars my dad owned so they were accustomed to considering those the best cars. Thinking of it now, I'm fascinated at how they were able to tell these cars apart from afar at elementary school age. This brings to mind the truth that our children often reflect our attitudes and values.

According to research from Pirchio (2020), "human beings, as all forms of living organisms, are shaped by the physical and social characteristics of their environment, which impact the development of their skills, preferences, habits, and behaviors."

On the other hand, individuals and social groups also leave a footprint on their habitats. The environment is, in some measure, an outcome of human actions. How parents react to the environment often shapes their children's attitude. One example of how parenting and the environment affects a child is the childhood of Jimmy Carter. In an interview with Oprah Winfrey on OWN TV, he said "I was the only white child in the whole neighborhood. My mother was a registered nurse who worked all night long, so I was raised by African American women, I grew up in the black culture, all my friends were African American."

His environment was shaped by human actions—parents who allowed him to play with black kids in the neighborhood. His mother amidst "strict lines of segregation in 1920s Georgia crossed the lines to counsel poor African-American women on matters of health care" (Strong, 2016). In his childhood, he played with children of a different race and his mother helped the community which was a different race without condemning those who were different.

Later in life, during his governorship campaign he surprised his white peers and political party with the line "the time for racial discrimination is over." He would later go on to "repeal laws designed to discourage African Americans from voting and increase the number of African American staff members in the Georgia government by 25 percent" (Strong, 2016b). He also launched the black college initiative for federal funding, and sparked several other controversial topics on race, segregation, and equality (*Ten Interesting Facts About Jimmy Carter's Civil Rights Record*, 2021). His views on race were shaped by his childhood experiences and his mother's attitude toward other races. This is true for all children, whether we are talking about a positive or a negative outcome. Parents and the environment make a huge difference in how a person views others as an adult. We need to be sure that we are raising children without prejudice for those who look differently than they do. We need to be sure that our children know that all people are created equal, all people have the same value.

Question

Do you think he would have done the same work for civil rights if he had grown up in a different neighborhood with different parents?

FOCUS ON YOUNGER GENERATION - Focusing on the younger generation is important. It needs to start early so the truth is entrenched in their sense of self and others. We must be cautious about what impressions we make on the next generation and the unintended messages and attitudes that we model. We need to encourage children to have friendship outside their circle, stay open to learning about their history, religion, and what makes other people different.

TV, the daily news stories, and the Internet has made it possible for everyone to be exposed to information that could have a negative effect. So, I will say yes to spending more time learning about history and how they can create change instead of creating Tik-Tok videos or spending all their time on the Internet. As many of you are aware, it is essential to know what your children are seeing and hearing on social media, news shows, and the entertainment industry. If you are not aware of available parental control apps, check them out. If you are, choose what works best for your family and use it to minimize the negative things your children are being exposed to. As children get older, they will be exposed to more negative ideas and attitudes. Discuss these ideas and guide your children to the truth. Limit content that does not support your moral standards until your child is old enough to discuss issues and make informed decisions. If we don't guide our children, there are plenty of other people willing to influence our children.

STRONGER IN TIMES OF ADVERSITY - History has shown that most "great advances in human rights and social progress occurred in the immediate aftermath of ..." (Morris, 2021) a life-threatening event beyond personal control. Morris highlighted some of the historic milestones achieved in a time like this. For example, the women's suffrage movement for the right to vote surged "in the wake of the devastation of World War I and the influenza pandemic of 1918."

History reports, the serfs in Europe had no hope of transitioning from servitude to becoming regular citizens and were treated inhumanly until the 14th century Black Death. The serfs were considered property along with the land that they lived and worked on. "The black death [bubonic plague] left much arable land uncultivated and also created an acute labor shortage, both economically favorable events for the peasantry." This resulted in freedom for serfs in Europe, forced wages for laborers to rise, and caused a fundamental shift in the economy along with an increased standard of living for survivors" of the pandemic (Magazine, 2018). https://www.britannica.com/event/Black-Death/Effects-and-significance

Perhaps there is a sudden realization of how similar we are in our vulnerability when disaster hits, prompting the sudden shift in perspective. After the pandemic is over, we need to continue helping others rather than revert to living a life for our individual gain alone.

Question

Reflecting on the many months of the pandemic, what actions did you take to help the vulnerable or contribute to you community? How do you plan to continue when things seem to normalize, and we are out of the pandemic? How do you plan to incorporate this action into your regular routine?

STILL GAPS TO FILL, DON'T STOP - On June 2, 2021, right after the stay-at-home order and mask restrictions began to ease, an ABC News report said: "Non-profit organizations seeing a shortage of volunteers which could impact the number of people served." As people begin to go back to work, they had less time to volunteer. As a result, organizations serving those in need are suffering from a lack of people to help.

LET'S DIALOGUE – Invoking a supportive nature takes a group effort. Encourage one another and speak up about ways that we could each become better individuals. For example, what makes a better chef is not always that he went to a better culinary school. It could simply be because he has taken advantage of feedback from customers, enabling him to refine his recipes and techniques learned at an average school. Being able to communicate genuinely to others about your expectations without anger and bias will create room to learn the true nature of the other person.

Hatred does the world no good, and we must take a stand to unite for our own good. Howard Thurman best put it together when he said, "hatred tends to dry out the spring of creative thoughts in the life of the hater so that his resourcefulness becomes focused on the negative aspects of his environment" (Thurman & Harding, 1996). If you have noticed those around you, it seems as if those who are the most negative and the most critical are the least content and happy with their life, their personal situation, and the world around them.

Matthew 5:44 instructs us to, "love your enemies and pray for those who persecute you." As I watch two random toddlers play at the park, I am struck by the fact they seem to be able to put aside differences and continue to play – as they fight over toys, laugh, chase after each other and wave each other goodbye as they leave without signs of the earlier fight. I believe hate is often born out of our life experiences, our environment and the notions we have created of the other based on our experiences and our peer group. In his book (*Jesus and the Disinherited 1996*),

Howard Thurman describes this formation of hate as, "hatred in the mind of the disinherited as one born out of great bitterness." Their experience has resulted in an attitude of hate and despair. Rich or poor, white or black, we need to do better. We can to better if we look to God to provide the strength and the wisdom needed to move past the hatred.

We must engage in grassroot conversations that cut across every age group inviting others to engage in constructive conversations on how we can maintain the same togetherness that we saw at the start of the pandemic. Taking initiatives and bringing people together "in a world that witnesses so much spiritual and moral decline, irrespective of faith, nationality, or ethnic group we can create much good" (Heaney et al., 2016).

D. Jomo

Chapter Eight
Invoking a Caring
Nature

*Service to others is the rent you pay for
your room here on Earth.*
Muhammad Ali

We cannot exist without each other.

I begin this book by emphasizing the importance of living and working together as one and realizing that we are more connected than we think we are. I also gave some accounts and events that exemplifies the life that we should embrace moving forward and those we need to eliminate. The pandemic has brought to light the fact that we need to think of others; that we must love our neighbor as our Creator teaches. Through God's Spirit, we can be our brother's keeper and live together in peace, loving our neighbor as we love ourselves.

The pandemic has helped millions realize the fragile nature of life and that we should nurture each day like a gift. We must leverage the awareness the pandemic brought to many of us to continue to work toward helping those who are less fortunate and providing equal opportunities for everyone.

Regardless of our faith, we have at some point come to the realization that life is a gift and that we did not play any role in our existence on earth. We had no role to play in how we were born, which parents and family we were born into, or even which country or continent we were born on. Each of us was given the gift of life. As a gift, we need to nurture and protect that gift for ourselves and for others.

Question

What has the pandemic taught you about the human nature?

COMING TO BEING -

The Bible says, "Now the earth was formless and empty, darkness was over the surface of the deep, and the Spirit of God was hovering over the water" (Genesis 1:1-2). It continues in Chapter 27: "So God created mankind in his own image, in the image of God He created them; male and female he created them."

We can argue that these verses do not explain the meaning of evolution to those in the 21st century, but until we find an answer accepted by both religious and non-religious groups, we can still live together knowing we do not agree. The religious view still stands in my opinion as no one has proven otherwise. In America we have freedom of religion. Everyone is entitled to their own opinion whether contrary to mine or not.

Whether a person believes in God and His creation of human beings in His likeness or whether they believe in evolution and the selection of the fittest, doesn't change the facts. Neither belief system suggests that we had anything to do with our arrival in this world.

So, the bottom line is that we have no power or control over our existence. Further, there is no escaping the truth that inequality of opportunity exists. There is much dissension over the degree of that inopportunity, but we all know that some people have more opportunities than others. There is no escaping the truth that there is much suffering among the peoples of the world, and we must do something to create change. We must come together to build a strong partnership with people different from ourselves to find solutions that are sustainable, solutions that give all people an opportunity to thrive and succeed.

D. Jomo

Nationwide Volunteer Organizations

Get matched to volunteer nationwide in any industry (the first five links are platforms with national volunteer data base nationwide).

Volunteer match - https://www.volunteermatch.org

United Way - https://www.unitedway.org/get-involved/volunteer

Volunteer.gov – https://www.voluteer.gov
Volunteers of America - https://www.voa.org/about-us

Americorp - https://americorps.gov/members-volunteers

Volunteer & Help Preserve Nature

National Park Services - https://www.nps.gov/getinvolved/volunteer.htm

National Oceanic and Atmospheric Administration - https://www.noaa.gov/work-with-us/volunteer-opportunities-citizen-scientists

U.S Fish & Wildlife Service - https://www.fws.gov/volunteer-opportunity

National River Cleanup

Ocean Conservancy

Zero Waste International Alliance

Volunteer by Helping Feed Others

Feed My Starving Children - https://www.fmsc.org

Feeding America - https://www.feedingamerica.org

Meals on Wheels America - https://www.mealsonwheelsamerica.org

In addition, most areas have local food banks that are always in need of donations and volunteers.

Volunteer with Kids

Adopt US Kids - https://www.adoptuskids.org/meet-the-children/search-for-children/search

Big Brothers, Big Sisters - https://www.bbbs.org

Nationwide Children - https://www.nationwidechildrens.org/giving/ways-to-give/volunteering

Reach Out & Read - https://reachoutandread.org/get-involved/volunteer/

Faith-based Volunteering

Catholic Relief Servies - https://www.crs.org/about/careers/volunteer-opportunities

Episcopal Community Services – https://www.ecscalifornia.org

Famvin Volunteers - https://famvin.help

Islamic Relief USA – https://iruas.org/volunteer/

Salvation Army Voluteers - https://www.salvationarmyusa.org/usn/volunteer/

Samaritan's Purse - https://www.samaritanspurse.org/what-we-do/volunteer/

There are many other faith-based organization that are not listed here. Most can be found with a Google search.

Community Building

American Red Cross - https://www.samaritanspurse.org/what-we-do/volunteer/

Arbor Day Foundation - https://www.arborday.org

FEMA (Federal Emergency Management Assistance) - https://www.fema.gov/disaster/recover/volunteer-donate

Grid Alternatives - https://gridalternatives.org/

Habitat for Humanity - https://www.habitat.org

The Food Project - https://thefoodproject.org

VITA (Volunteer Income Tax Assistance - IRS volunteer tax preparer) https://www.irs.gov/individuals/irs-tax-volunteers

Mental Health Organizations

American Foundation for Suicide Prevention – https://afsp.org

MHA (Mental Health America) https://www.mhanational.org

National Alliance on Mental Health https://nami.org

References

The 1918–19 Spanish Influenza Pandemic and Vaccine Development | History of Vaccines. (n.d.). History of Vaccines. Retrieved September 20, 2021, from https://www.historyofvaccines.org/content/blog/vaccine-development-spanish-flu

"Absolutely Unacceptable" Vaccination Rates in Developing Countries. (2021, July 30). World Bank. https://www.worldbank.org/en/news/podcast/2021/07/30/-absolutely-unacceptable-vaccination-rates-in-developing-countries-the-development-podcast

Atske, S., & Perrin, A. (2021, July 16). *Home broadband adoption, computer ownership vary by race, ethnicity in the U.S.* Pew Research Center. https://www.pewresearch.org/fact-tank/2021/07/16/home-broadband-adoption-computer-ownership-vary-by-race-ethnicity-in-the-u-s/

Beyer W., (1968). *Individual Freedom in a Collective Society.*https://fisher.osu.edu/blogs/leadreadtoday/blog/leadership-tip-of-the-week-i-versus-we#:~:text=As%20a%20leader%2C%20use%20%E2%80%9CI,Dawson's%20paper%20on%20narcissistic%20leaders).

Brito C. (2020). *Spring Breakers Say Coronavirus Pandemic Won't Stop Them From Partying.* https://www.cbsnews.com/news/spring-break-party-coronavirus-pandemic-miami-beaches/

Capehart, J. (2020, June 10). *John Lewis to Black Lives Matter protesters: 'Give until you cannot give any more.* Washington Post. https://www.washingtonpost.com/opinions/2020/06/10/ john-lewis-black-lives-matter-protesters-give-until-you- cannot-give-any-more/

CNBC. (June 9, 2020). *CNBC Asked, you Nominated: The Brave Compassionate Heroes of the Coronavirus Pandemic.* https://www.cnbc.com/2020/06/09/cnbc-recognizes- coronavirus-heroes-for-bravery-compassion-in- pandemic.html

Cunningham, E. (2018, April 6). *Great Recession, great recovery? Trends from the Current Population Survey : Monthly Labor Review: U.S. Bureau of Labor Statistics.* U.S. BURAEU OF LABOR STATISTICS. https://www.bls.gov/opub/mlr/2018/article/great- recession-great-recovery.htm

Ellis, R. (1993). *American Political Cultures.* New York: Oxford University Press.

Global Inequality. (2021, July 8). Inequality.Org. https://inequality.org/facts/global-inequality/

Goodnough, A., & Hoffman, J. (2021, March 4). *Even in Poorer Neighborhoods, the Wealthy Are Lining Up for Vaccines.* The New York Times. https://www.nytimes.com/2021/02/02/health/white- people-covid-vaccines-minorities.html

Heaney, R. S., Sayilgan, Z., & Haymes, C. (2016). *Faithful Neighbors.* Van Haren Publishing.

Hittler, J. (2018, August 2). *Why Learning To Unlearn Is So Important*. Forbes. https://www.forbes.com/sites/forbescoachescouncil/201 8/08/02/why-learning-to-unlearn-is-so-important/?sh=72d295382444

Holder, J. (2021, October 4). *Covid World Vaccination Tracker*. The New York Times. https://www.nytimes.com/interactive/2021/world/covid -vaccinations-tracker.html

India | United States Trade Representative. (n.d.). Office of the United States Trade Representative. Retrieved September 20, 2021, from https://ustr.gov/countries-regions/south-central-asia/india

Joo, N. A. R. R. V. (2017, November 3). *White, still: The American upper middle class*. Brookings. https://www.brookings.edu/blog/social-mobility-memos/2017/10/04/white-still-the-american-upper-middle-class/

Kats, Y. (2014). *The tombstone in Israel's military cemetery since 1948: Israel's transition from collectivism to individualism.*

Magazine, S. (2018, March 2). *How the 1918 Flu Pandemic Helped Advance Women's Rights*. Smithsonian Magazine. https://www.smithsonianmag.com/history/how-1918-flu-pandemic-helped-advance-womens-rights-180968311/

Masuda, N. (2015). Faculty Opinions recommendation of Birds of a feather: homophily in social networks. *Faculty*

Opinions – Post-Publication Peer Review of the Biomedical Literature. Published. https://doi.org/10.3410/f.725356294.793504070

McPherson, M., Smith-Lovin, L., & Cook, J. M. (2001). Birds of a Feather: Homophily in Social Networks. *Annual Review of Sociology*, *27*(1), 415–444. https://doi.org/10.1146/annurev.soc.27.1.415

Meeks, C. (2016). *Living into God's Dream: Dismantling Racism in America*. Morehouse Publishing.

Merelli, A. (2021, June 8). *Rich countries are buying up all the Covid-19 vaccines*. Quartz. https://qz.com/2017272/rich-countries-are-buying-up-all-the-covid-19-vaccines/

Morris, P. (2021, May 3). *2020 has tested our humanity. Where do we go from here?* Magazine. https://www.nationalgeographic.com/magazine/article/2020-has-tested-our-humanity-where-do-we-go-from-here-feature

Office of the Commissioner. (2021, September 23). *FDA Authorizes Booster Dose of Pfizer-BioNTech COVID-19 Vaccine for Certain Populations*. U.S. Food and Drug Administration. https://www.fda.gov/news-events/press-announcements/fda-authorizes-booster-dose-pfizer-biontech-covid-19-vaccine-certain-populations

Peterson-Withorn, C. (2021, April 30). *How Much Money America's Billionaires Have Made During The Covid-19 Pandemic*. Forbes. https://www.forbes.com/sites/chasewithorn/2021/04/30/

american-billionaires-have-gotten-12-trillion-richer-during-the-pandemic/?sh=3d09eb0bf557

Pirchio, S. (2020). *Editorial: Where to Raise Happy and Skilled Children: How Environment Shapes Human Development and Education.* Frontiers. https://www.frontiersin.org/articles/10.3389/fpsyg.2020 .594924/full

Ritchie, H. (2020, March 5). *Coronavirus (COVID-19) Vaccinations - Statistics and Research.* Our World in Data. https://ourworldindata.org/covid-vaccinations

Smith N. (2020). *"A Team of Five Million." How new Zealand Best Corona Virus.* Direct Relief. https://www.directrelief.org/2020/08/a-team-of-5-million-how-new-zealand-beat-coronavirus/

Steinhauser, G., & Hinshaw, D. (2021, April 27). *India's Covid-19 Agonies Highlight Growing Rich-Poor Gap in Vaccinations.* WSJ. https://www.wsj.com/articles/indias-covid-19-agonies-highlight-growing-rich-poor-gap-in-vaccinations-11619542171

Strong, R. A. (2016, October 4). *Jimmy Carter: Life Before the Presidency.* Miller Center. https://millercenter.org/president/carter/life-before-the-presidency

Ten Interesting Facts About Jimmy Carter's Civil Rights Record. (2021, March 11). ThoughtCo. https://www.thoughtco.com/president-jimmy-carters-civil-rights-record-2834612

The Physical Environment and Child Development: An International Review. (2013) Published. https://doi.org/10.1080/00207594.2013.804190

Thurman, H., & Harding, V. (1996). *Jesus and the Disinherited* (Reprint ed.). Beacon Press.

Trends in income and wealth inequality. (2020, May 30). Pew Research Center's Social & Demographic Trends Project. https://www.pewresearch.org/social-trends/2020/01/09/trends-in-income-and-wealth-inequality/

Triandis, H. (1995). *Individualism & collectivism* (New directions in social psychology). Boulder, Colo.: Oxford: Westview.

Why Having Friends That Don't Look Like You Is Important. (2021, February 27). Verywell Mind. https://www.verywellmind.com/why-it-s-important-to-diversify-your-friendships-5072980

About the Author

Daphne Jomo has always believed in the need to help others with a soft spot in her heart for seniors who are in need of companionship. During the COVID-19 pandemic, as needs for services ballooned, she became aware of many areas that marginalized people were in need. She wants to share what she learned with the goal of making others aware of needs and ways to help. A graduate of the University of South Sewanee, she feels the world can do better in helping and respecting all others.

Made in United States
North Haven, CT
25 April 2023

35872095R00065